curious about

GOBLINS

BY GINA KAMMER

AMICUS LEARNING

What

curious about?

CHAPTER THREE

Finding Goblins

Curious About is published by
Amicus Learning, an imprint of Amicus
P.O. Box 227
Mankato, MN 56002
www.amicuspublishing.us

Editor: Ana Brauer
Series Designer: Kathleen Petelinsek
Book Designer and Photo Researcher: Kim Pfeffer

Library of Congress Cataloging-in-Publication Data
Names: Kammer, Gina, author.
Title: Curious about goblins / by Gina Kammer.
Description: Mankato, MN : Amicus Learning, [2025] | Series: Curious about mythical creatures | Includes bibliographical references and index. | Audience: Ages 6–9 years | Audience: Grades 2–3 | Summary: "Are goblins friendly? Learn about the mythology surrounding goblins in this question-and-answer book for elementary readers. Includes infographics, table of contents, glossary, books and websites for further research, and index"— Provided by publisher.
Identifiers: LCCN 2024017583 | ISBN 9798892000970 (lib. bdg.) | ISBN 9798892001557 (paperback) | ISBN 9798892002134 (ebook)
Subjects: LCSH: Goblins—Juvenile literature.
Classification: LCC GR549 .K363 2025 | DDC 398.21—dc23/eng/20240529
LC record available at https://lccn.loc.gov/2024017583

Photos © Adobe Stock/Ash, 21 (middle), Eduardo, 21 (bottom), Hanna Haradzetska, 12–13, 16–17, LayerAce.com, 5, 15 (top), Ravi, 11; Alamy Stock Photo/RGR Collection, 21 (top), SOPA Images, 21 (second from top); Flickr/Andrea Alemanno, 15 (right); Freep!k/EyeEm, 20, gndesign, 6, sergeyparser, cover; Pixabay/pendleburyannette, 21 (second from bottom); Public Domain/unknown, 9; Wikimedia Commons/John Dickson Batten, 15 (left), Public Domain, 18–19, Winifred Knights, 4

Printed in China

CHAPTER ONE

What are goblins?

In one poem, goblins trick a young woman into eating fruit that makes her sick. The woman's sister saves her.

Goblins are **evil** or tricky creatures. Some might be spirits or **demons**. In old stories, they might be scary monsters. In others, they are just **sprites** that cause trouble. Usually, goblins are a type of fairy. But they don't look like fairies!

A lot of people imagine goblins as being green with pointed ears.

Are goblins real?

In stories, some goblins like to get into trouble while others hide from humans.

Who can tell? Has something of yours ever gone missing? Did your milk suddenly spill? Maybe it was a goblin! They don't let people see them. Goblins appear in many stories. But there is no **proof** that they're real.

Many cultures have goblin stories. They have similar powers. But they all have different names.

What do goblins look like?

Goblins are similar to humans but uglier! Yellow, sharp teeth and pointy ears make them scary. Their skin is green, tan, or gray in color. Some have wide, sturdy bodies. Some are thin. Many wear gray clothes with red caps.

In one tale, humans went to war against goblins that were stealing children.

COMPARING SIZES

How big are goblins?

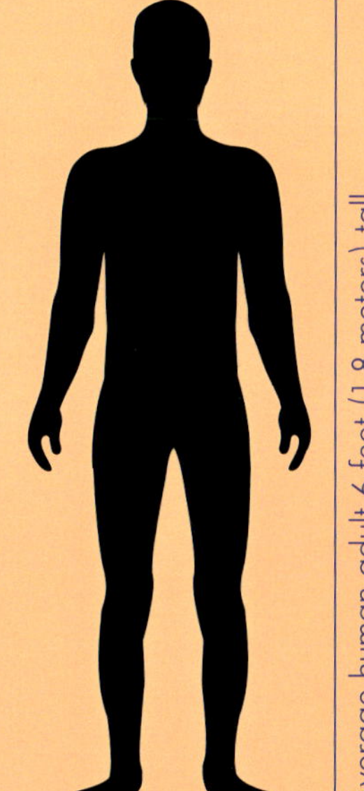

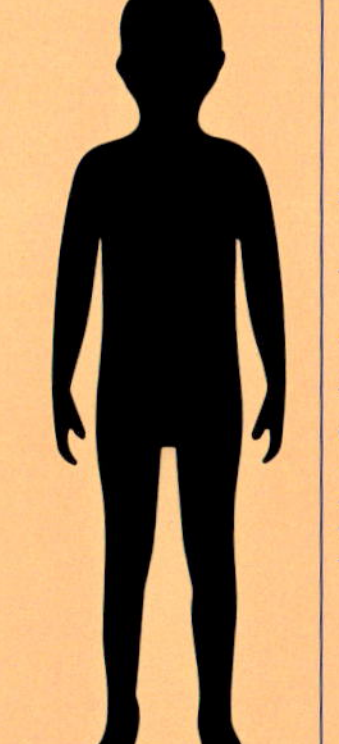

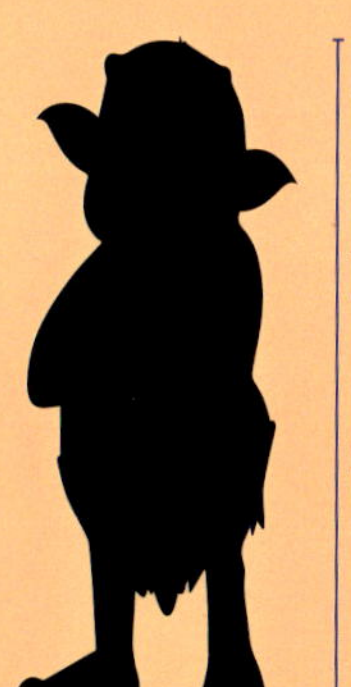

What magic powers do goblins have?

They're **sly**! Goblins can turn invisible so people can't see them. Then they can play tricks. Some change shapes. House goblins might protect the home and family living there. Other goblins cause nightmares. Goblins called Redcaps can fight with weapons called pikes.

In stories and art, goblins are often shown to be greedy creatures.

Depending on the myth, goblins will eat anything from mushrooms to cream to rats.

What do goblins like to do?

Some like poetry. They love to eat cream. Some goblins pick a home to stay in. If the family is nice, it may help with chores when no one is watching. If the family makes the goblin angry, it causes trouble. Goblins bang on walls or pans. Food burns. Clothes go missing.

Are goblins friendly?

It depends on the goblin! Some steal children and hurt people. But others aren't usually as scary. Still, it would be wise not to make a goblin angry. They like to pay people back with mean tricks. Keep a goblin happy by leaving out food.

Hobgoblins are known for being helpful around the house.

TYPES OF GOBLINS

HOBGOBLIN:
smaller, friendlier, house goblin

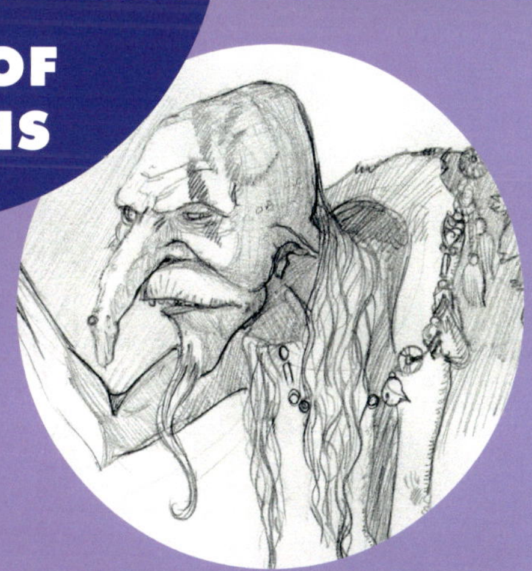

GOBLIN:
larger, meaner, lives underground

Where do goblins live?

Goblins are quick and sneaky. They can be hard to find.

According to legend, goblins live underground. They have homes in caves with tunnels. But some like to find a house to stay in. There are also goblins that move into mines or ships. If the crew keeps them happy, goblins will protect the ship.

Can goblins do my chores?

A goblin is more likely to help someone who is nice to it.

Maybe! They might help if you leave some bread and cream by your stove. Add lots of butter. Goblins need to eat to work. Goblins want smart people to say nice things about them. Try reading at home so a goblin can spy on you. It'll know how smart you are!

What else could a goblin be?

There are about 652,000 people with dwarfism around the world.

Some people are born with **dwarfism**. Goblins are usually short. Long ago, people may not have known about the **condition**. Maybe they made up ideas about what people with dwarfism could be. Miners also told stories about goblins. They sometimes saw strange things under the ground.

THE SPIDERWICK CHRONICLES – GOBLINS, HOBGOBLINS
HARRY POTTER – BANKER GOBLINS
DISCWORLD – MECHANIC RACE OF GOBLINS
THE HOBBIT – MISTY MOUNTAIN GOBLINS
DUNGEONS AND DRAGONS – GOBLINS, BUGBEARS

STAY CURIOUS!

ASK MORE QUESTIONS

What stories have people told about goblins?

What do different cultures call goblins?

Try a BIG QUESTION: Why might some people leave out food or other things for goblins?

SEARCH FOR ANSWERS

Search the library catalog or the Internet.
A librarian, teacher, or parent can help you.

Using Keywords
Find the looking glass.

Keywords are the most important words in your question.

If you want to know about

- Goblins in fairy tales, type: GOBLIN FAIRY TALES
- Goblins in other cultures, type: GOBLINS ACROSS CULTURES

LEARN MORE

FIND GOOD SOURCES

Are the sources reliable?
Some sources are better than others. An adult can help you. Here are some good, safe sources.

Books

Fairy Tale Creatures: Goblins
by Emma Huddleston, 2022.

The Book of Mythical Beasts and Magical Creatures
by Stephen Krensky, 2020.

Internet Sites

National Geographic Kids: Goblin Shark
https://kids.nationalgeographic.com/animals/fish/facts/goblin-shark
National Geographic is an organization based on science.

Nemours KidsHealth: Dwarfism
https://kidshealth.org/en/kids/emily-story.html
Nemours teaches about health topics and is reviewed by doctors.

SHARE AND TAKE ACTION

Go to your library, and find books with goblin stories.
Read about how goblins are shown differently in different tales.

What lives underground?
Find out what makes tunnels or lives in caves like goblins.

Make your own goblin cave.
Make a fort with friends, or family, and use cardboard boxes to build tunnels.

GLOSSARY

condition A state of fitness.

demon A spirit that wants to hurt people.

dwarfism A condition in which people or animals are much smaller than average.

evil Something or someone bad or cruel that wants to hurt others.

proof Facts or evidence that show something is true.

sly Acting in a clever way to trick people.

sprite A small creature with magic powers that likes to play tricks.

INDEX

About the Author

Gina Kammer grew up writing and illustrating her own stories. Now she teaches others to write stories at inkybookwyrm.com. She likes reading fantasy and medieval literature. She also enjoys traveling, oil painting, archery, and snuggling her grumpy bunny. She lives in Minnesota.